D0623244

The 2000–2002 Forest Fires in the Western United States

Katherine White

The Rosen Publishing Group, Inc., New York

Published in 2004 by The Rosen Publishing Group, Inc.
29 East 21st Street, New York, NY 10010

Library of Congress Cataloging-in-Publication Data

White, Katherine.
The 2000-2002 forest fires in the western United States / Katherine White.— 1st ed.
     p. cm. — (Tragic fires throughout history)
Includes bibliographical references (p.   ).
Contents: The fury of forest fires — Fire seasons 2000 and 2001 — Fire season 2002: Washington, California, and Oregon — Fire Season 2002: Colorado, Utah, and Arizona.
ISBN 0-8239-4488-3 (library binding)
1. Forest fires—West (U.S.)—History—Juvenile literature. 2. Forest fires—West (U.S.)—Prevention and control—History—Juvenile literature. [1. Forest fires—West (U.S.)] I. Title: Two thousand-two thousand two fires in the western United States. II. Title. III. Series.
SD421.32.W47W55 2003
634.9'618'0978--dc22
                              2003018134

Manufactured in the United States of America

CONTENTS

Introduction

Every May through September, forest fires rage throughout the western United States. From New Mexico to Washington and from Arizona to Idaho, sparks fly and smoke swirls. Small flames move across the forest floor, growing stronger as they come upon natural fuels, such as dry leaves, scattered sticks, and fallen timber. Heavy smoke begins to rise. Sitting high up in a watchtower that rises over the trees, a lookout person sees the black plume rising above the treetops. He or she sends out an alert to firefighters, hoping to catch the fire in its early stages, when it can still be controlled.

The smokejumpers are the first firefighters on the scene. They parachute from airplanes, carrying shovels and chain saws. They get their name from their air delivery. If they succeed in digging deep trenches in time to control the flames, disaster can be avoided. If the smokejumpers don't succeed, aerial firefighters are called in. These firefighters fly large planes, called air tankers, over the burning forest and drop tons of water and retardant, a chemical mixture that helps slow or stop fires from spreading. Air tankers are like fire engines in the sky. The aerial firefighters have a strategy: drop the water and retardant mixture on the fire, drown it, and smother the flames. Very often, the 1,200 gallons (4,542 liters) of water and retardant dropped from the air tankers snap off the tops of trees.

Captain Brett Haring of the Woodbridge, California, fire department scans the flames of the Hayman Fire near Trumbull, Colorado in 2002. The lenses of his binoculars are tinted pink to eliminate the fire's glare.

If the flames rage on, then the hotshots are called in. They arrive in yellow uniforms. Their job is to build fire lines and firebreaks—deep gullies that surround the blaze and contain it. These firefighters go into the forest and set up camps, moving into the flames to combat them. At the same time, a command post comes alive and hums with information from weather satellites. Where is the fire heading? Which way is the wind blowing? Is rain expected? Are there other fires nearby that could merge with this one? Are the ground and aerial crews safe? These answers are key to containing a forest fire.

The fire spreads. The forest lights up. This is only the beginning. There are homes to protect. What about the people who live in them? They may evacuate or wait it out, hoping the fire will not destroy their homes. There are also forest animals losing their homes. The firefighters put their lives in danger to save the people, the animals, and the forest. Everyone wants the firefighters to gain control so the fire can be put out quickly. The faster the fire is put out, the less damage there is.

Days fly by, then weeks, as whole teams of firefighters, air tankers, helicopters, and ground crews swarm around the fire, fighting it, pushing their bodies and their skills to the limit. Success comes when the fire is put out. Only then can the ground firefighters and aerial firefighters feel that their job is complete. After a blaze is out, firefighters do not go home. Instead, they move on to the next fire. During fire season, there are always more fires to fight and more forests to save.

The Fury of Forest Fires

Every year wildfires destroy about 5 million acres (about 2 million hectares) of forest throughout the United States. In 2002, Colorado, Arizona, and Oregon recorded their largest forest fires in the last century. Statistics show that these states are not alone; forest fires are on the rise across the country. Firefighters and fire scientists, called fire ecologists, are learning better ways to fight forest fires, but forest fires are happening more often and are also getting larger.

According to the National Interagency Fire Center (NIFC), from 2000 to 2002 almost 300,000 fires burned the western United States. All of these fires burned close to a combined 19 million acres (7.7 million ha) of forest. An acre is about the size of a football field; 19 million acres is about the size of South Carolina. The big question for scientists is why forest fires are becoming an increasing problem. With better research, technology, and firefighting, shouldn't forest fires be less of a problem? The answer should be yes. The problem is that most forest fires do not start naturally.

When left unattended, campfires can burn out of control. It's important to make sure that campfires are built away from trees, pine needles on the forest floor, and other flammable materials.

How Forest Fires Begin

Most forest fires begin because people are careless. In fact, nine out of ten forest fires are caused by humans. In some cases, campers leave their campfires unattended and the fire spreads while no one is paying attention. Other times, people burn debris or carelessly throw lit cigarettes or matches onto the forest floor. Arson is when a person starts a fire intentionally. In a strange case in 2002, a Colorado forest worker named Terry Barton burned a love letter from her ex-husband. The burning letter started a forest fire called the Hayman Fire. The fire burned 137,760 acres (55,749 ha), destroyed 133 homes, and cost more than $39 million to fight. This fire is discussed in more detail in chapter three.

Mother Nature's Fire Starters

Lightning is also a big cause of forest fires. Lightning occurs in two stages. First, an invisible strike, or leader, is sent from a thundercloud. When the leader reaches the ground, a return series of strikes travels back up, meeting the leader and producing the visible flash of light that we know as a lightning bolt. When lightning hits any object, the heat produced can spark a fire. When lightning strikes in a forest, a forest fire can begin. Even though lightning is a big cause of forest fires, carelessness on the part of humans still causes many more fires. The NIFC reports that from 1988 to 1997, people caused 102,694 forest fires, while lightning caused just 13,879 forest fires.

What Is Fire Season?

Forest fires are actually beneficial to the environment. For thousands of years, natural fires have been

Lightning is the greatest natural cause of forest fires.

LARGE FOREST FIRES OF THE 1990s

Name and Date	Location	Acres Burned
South Blaine County October 1991	Washington	181,000 (73,248 hectares)
Foothills August 1992	Idaho	257,000 (104,004 ha)
Idaho City Complex July 1994	Idaho	154,000 (62,322 ha)
Cox Wells August 1996	Idaho	219,000 (88,626 ha)
Inowak July 1997	Alaska	610,000 (246,858 ha)
Dunn Glen Complex August 1999	Nevada	288,220 (116,638 ha)
Big Bar Complex August–November 1999	California	140,947 (57,039 ha)
Kirk Complex September–November 1999	California	86,700 (35,086 ha)

burning as a way to keep a balanced ecosystem. An ecosystem is a community of plants and animals living together. Forest fires trigger regrowth in forests by burning dead wood and excess tangled brush. Fires can also kill off diseases that may be damaging a forest. After a forest fire, the forest goes through a period of rebirth that helps some species. Forest fires help thin forests, clearing away too much vegetation that can crowd out certain plants and trees. Without smaller, natural forest fires occurring periodically, extra vegetation (fallen leaves, small timber, and plants) will build up and eventually feed enormous and uncontrollable forest fires.

The fire season is part of the natural cycle. It happens every May through September in the western United States. Though fire season is natural, unnatural causes are making the fire season bigger—and more dangerous—than it should be.

Causes for Forest Fires Increase

If forest fires are needed to balance an ecosystem, then why is the increase in forest fires so bad? Forest fires are only effective, or helpful, when they help balance the ecosystem. The unusual increase of forest fires in the past twenty years has not helped the ecosystem; it has actually harmed it. Forest fires destroy vegetation that is food and shelter for animals that live in and around the forest. With too many fires, a forest is unable to start over, throwing the delicate ecosystem out of balance.

What exactly is causing the rise? Both nature and people. Smokeybear.com reports three main reasons why forest fires are on the rise: fire policies, dry weather, and more people in the forests.

Fire Policies

A fire suppression policy is a plan of action to fight fires. Scientists and firefighters create and use these policies to prevent, combat, and learn from forest fires. In the past, one of the policies was "total suppression." This policy worked to rid forests of all forest fires, before they even began. The problem with this approach is that forest fires actually need to happen to keep a balanced ecosystem. During the total suppression policy, more fire fuels were stored up in forests. The excess fallen leaves, branches, and plant growth that normally would have been consumed in small fires eventually led to bigger fires than ever before.

Dry Weather

For many years, scientists said that the earth's weather patterns were changing. The rise in forest fires supports this idea. Summers are increasingly dry and extra hot. The rise in temperature causes droughts across the United States. With less rain, forests become drier, and forest fires start and spread more easily.

More People in the Forests

As the world becomes more populated, more people are building homes and starting neighborhoods in areas surrounded by forests.

This home is directly in the path of a fire as it advances through Durango, Colorado. For many people, evacuating their homes is the only option when wildfires grow too large to control.

This means more people interact with the forest, and they often unbalance the forest's natural ecosystem. Also, this increases the chances of fires being started by human carelessness.

Scientists and Politicians Fight Back

In 2000, the administration of President Clinton decided to take action against forest fires. Firefighters and firefighter associations throughout the United States brought forest fires to the government's attention. They said there was a dangerous lack of

This Smokey the Bear sign is planted in the San Juan Mountains of Colorado. Smokey's well-known motto, "Only you can prevent forest fires," encourages campers to take responsibility for fire prevention.

knowledge about and resources for fighting forest fires. In 2000 alone, nearly 8 million acres (3.2 million ha) burned, a staggering number that the federal government could not ignore. As a result, the National Fire Plan was established. The project was given $1.8 billion a year to strengthen resources—for hiring more firefighters, buying better equipment, and increasing research to getting the community involved in fire prevention.

Under the National Fire Plan, scientists study ways to make it easier to monitor how much fuel a fire has, to track weather patterns, and to predict climate changes. The sudden changes in weather that spark and fuel forest fires are intensely studied. The National Fire Plan also has restoration and rehabilitation initiatives that focus on helping the forest recover after it has burned. The final two aspects of the National Fire Plan are hazardous fuel reduction and community assistance. Reducing hazardous fuels is a big part of helping a forest grow back healthily after a fire. Finally, getting the community involved is vitally important because it helps cut down on forest fires and helps communities bounce back after a forest fire. The biggest goal of the National Forest Plan is to restore the natural relationship between forests and forest fires by allowing fire to balance ecosystems.

Fire Seasons
2000 and 2001

In 2000, the western United States was lit up with thousands of forest fires that burned 8 million acres (3.2 million ha) of land. That's twice the ten-year average of acres burned. With the recently installed National Fire Plan in effect, the 2001 fire season saw a more usual amount of forest fires with nearly 3.6 million acres (1.5 million ha) of land burned. Some of the largest and most challenging forest fires from 2000 and 2001 were in Idaho, Montana, Colorado, and Washington.

Clear Creek Fire, Idaho, 2000

On July 8, 2000, during a summer thunderstorm in Idaho, lightning strikes sparked a forest fire. The lightning hit a very dry and remote area in Clear Creek, Idaho, part of the Salmon-Challis National Forest. After starting as a small fire, the blaze grew for two days before it was spotted. It took ninety minutes for crews to get to the fire, and by then 10 more acres (4 ha) had burned. It was particularly windy that day, and the flames spread rapidly thanks to the 25 mph (40.2 km/h) gusts. By the next morning, the fire had eaten up 30 more acres (12 ha) of forest. Firefighters were inside the forest battling the fire, but they could not get it under control. By nightfall, the fire had grown to nearly 200 acres (81 ha).

Almost one week into battling the blaze, on July 14, the wind picked up to 50 mph (80.5 km/h), which spread the wildfire even faster. By July 18, the fire was outrageous—blazing 39,000 acres (15,783 ha)—and getting worse. By July 23, 800 firefighters were on the scene, and the fire was still growing. Two months later, the Clear Creek Fire was at its peak, engulfing almost 206,500 acres (83,568 ha) of forest. By August 30, 1,787 people, sixteen helicopters, forty-seven fire engines, and twenty bulldozers were on the scene. On October 13, the fire was finally contained. Temperatures had dropped and some snow fell, which finally made the fire manageable.

Bitterroot Valley Fires, Montana, 2000

On July 31, 2000, Hamilton, Montana, experienced major thunder-storms. The lightning from the storms set off almost sixty fires in southwestern Montana. One of the lightning bolts hit an area in the Bitterroot Valley and another hit Mussigbrod, both in Montana. The fires moved through the forests and quickly grew out of control.

A week later, on August 6, the two fires combined to make one enormous blaze. By then, the fire was at 247,000 acres (99,958 ha), and most of the small mountain villages around the fire were

CONTAINING A FOREST FIRE

After firefighters have built a fire line around the perimeter of a fire, the fire is considered contained. Interestingly, fire lines can be man-made or natural, meaning they can be rivers and roads rather than just the deep trenches and firebreaks that firefighters dig. When the initial fire line is strong enough that the fire cannot jump it or when all the spot fires (smaller fires around the larger fire) are out, then the fire is controlled. During the "mop-up" phase, firefighters go inside the fire line and put out all the hot spots and burning embers.

evacuated. By August 28, the fires had destroyed seventy homes. "This is the biggest fire complex in the region," Lynn Burkett of the National Interagency Fire Center told CNN. "[W]ith a fire of that size and magnitude, it will take a significant fall weather event to stop it—like rain or snow."

In the end, the Bitterroot Valley Fires burned more than 300,000 acres (121,406 ha) and cost $54 million to fight.

Bobcat Gulch and Hi Meadows Fires, Colorado, 2000

In the foothills of the Rocky Mountains near Denver, two forest fires broke out on June 12, 2000. The Bobcat Gulch Fire was started by an illegal campfire. Meanwhile, a lightning strike started the Hi Meadows Fire. Both fires spread incredibly fast due to unseasonably

Using Pulaskis, firefighting tools that have an ax head on one side and a hoe on the other, these firefighters work hard to create a fire line. They are hoping to bring a fire in Payette National Forest in Idaho under control.

warm, dry weather and a lack of rain. By the second day of the Bobcat Gulch Fire, the blaze was spreading one mile each hour, and flames were shooting 100 to 150 feet (30 to 46 meters) above the treetops.

Mark Michelsen is the manager at the Jeffco Airtanker Base near Denver. Michelsen's job includes managing the air tanker base and aerial retardant programs, receiving air tanker requests during fires, dispatching air tankers, and coordinating air tanker loading, fueling, and parking at the base. Michelsen has nearly a decade of experience fighting forest fires, both as a ground firefighter and as

MARK MICHELSEN

Mark Michelsen will always remember his work as a ground firefighter. In an interview, he explained that his experience fighting fire on the ground actually helps him as he works with air tankers: "My experience as a 'ground-pounder' gives me the insight to be more effective in my operations. My crews and I go to great lengths to provide the best support to the crew on the ground. We provide a tool to make their jobs easier and more effective. Working the fire line is hard, dauntless work, and I have never forgotten what it's like to be there."

an aerial firefighter. In a recent interview, he explained why the Bobcat Gulch and Hi Meadows Fires were two of the most challenging of his career: "Both of these very large fires started within one hour of each other and grew to type 1 incidents—highest priority and complexity. With our base comfortably working four air tankers at any given time, I had to manage and coordinate nine tankers, going seven days a week, roughly fourteen to sixteen hours a day, with daily temperatures into the low 100s and high 90s."

Michelsen explained that hot, dry weather—which helps spread the fire—was not the only thing that made these two fires a challenge. He also said, "During the time of these fires, we had multiple small fires that had started as well. In simple terms, we had to kind of play leapfrog while going from fire to fire."

The Bobcat Gulch and Hi Meadows Fires were almost under control by June 21, but the damage from both was extreme. According to the United States Department of Agriculture (USDA) Forest Service, the Hi Meadows Fire burned nearly 11,000 acres (4,454 ha) and destroyed fifty-eight structures, including fifty-one homes. The Bobcat Gulch Fire burned around 10,000 acres (4,047 ha) and consumed twenty-two buildings. The total cost of fighting the fires was between $15 and $19 million.

This image taken on June 16, 2000, from the *IKONOS* satellite shows smoke rising from burned stretches of forest in Colorado, which are colored dark blue.

The Thirtymile Fire, Washington, 2001

Temperatures in southeastern Washington on July 9, 2001, were more than 100°F (37.8°C). Thirty miles (48.3 km) north of Winthrop, Washington, in the Okanogan National Forest, a small cooking fire at a picnic went out of control. High temperatures, low humidity, and a severe drought caused the fire to spread quickly.

By the next day, the fire had spread from a 25-acre (10-ha) blaze to 8,200 acres (3,318 ha). Firefighters were on the scene and making

This memorial near Winthrop, Washington, stands in memory of four firefighters who died fighting the Thirtymile Fire on July 10, 2001.

progress when disaster struck. Fourteen firefighters and two hikers were trapped late that afternoon by the fire along the Chewuch River. According to an August 1, 2001, article in the *Seattle Times*, "[D]ispatchers delayed sending a helicopter to drop water on the flames because they were unsure whether they needed permission to draw water from a river containing threatened fish, the U.S. Forest Service said." Four firefighters lost their lives: Tom Craven, Karen FitzPatrick, Jessica Johnson, and Devin Weaver. The fire was put out by July 24, but the tragic loss of the four firefighters has spurred a lot of debate about firefighting strategies during the Thirtymile Fire.

Lakeview Complex Fire, Oregon 2001

On August 9, 2001, lightning sparked a forest fire on the northeast side of Big Juniper Mountain in Oregon. That storm also started the Johnson Creek, South Warner, Mustang, and Horsehead Fires. All of the fires together were named the Lakeview Complex Fire. The fires burned a total of 127,552 acres (51,618 ha) in just seven days—an incredibly fast fire spread. Amazingly, Oregon firefighters had this fire 100 percent contained by September 3, 2001.

Overview of Fire Season 2000 and 2001

In 2000, the NIFC reported "a pool of cold water in the Pacific Ocean had been affecting weather across the United States for the past two

CROWN FIRES: THE HARDEST FIRES TO FIGHT

A crown fire is when a forest fire leaps from treetop to treetop, spreading rapidly across the forest. Crown fires are extremely hard to fight because they are incredibly hot and produce high winds. According to a *Scientific American* article entitled "Burning Questions," "Not only can crown fires easily cross a five-foot [1.5-m] firebreak scratched out by crews . . . they have been known to hurdle rivers hundreds of feet wide." Crown fires can shoot flames 400 feet (122 m) into the air and can cause temperatures to rise enormously, up to 2,000°F (1,093°C).

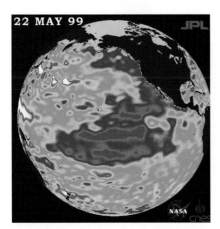

22 MAY 99   JPL
NASA

The purple areas in this satellite image show where the sea level has fallen in the wake of La Niña.

years. This weather pattern, called 'La Niña,' was at its strongest in the late winter/early spring of 2000. As a result of La Niña and its influence on weather patterns, a combination of dry fuels and dry, hot weather led to what some are declaring one of the most serious wildland fire seasons in U.S. history."

The 2000 wildland fire season began in January, became intense very fast, and lasted longer than usual. Fires began in mid-February in New Mexico, and by mid-July, most western states reported a number of large fires. The NIFC declared a planning level of 5—the highest possible. According to the NIFC, by August 5, more than 30,000 people, including civilian firefighters, the National Guard, the U.S. Army and Marines, and rural fire departments were on fire lines or supporting fires in eleven western states. A total of 8 million acres (3.2 million ha) burned.

In comparison, the 2001 wildland fire season was pretty typical—around 4 million acres (1.6 million ha) burned. Some areas of the West had worse seasons, though, like Washington and Oregon. In fact, the NIFC reported, "Florida, Nevada, Washington, and Oregon accounted for almost half [1.6 of the 3.5 million] of the acres burned nationwide."

Fire Season 2002: Washington, California, and Oregon

The 2002 fire season was one of the worst in the past fifty years, second only to the 2000 fire season. According to the NIFC, there were 88,458 forest fires during the 2002 fire season, and they burned more than 7 million acres (2.8 million ha). Together, the fires cost an astounding $1.6 billion to fight. While California and Washington experienced major forest fires, Oregon had even larger fires, recording the state's biggest forest fires in more than a century.

Deer Point Fire, Washington

On July 15, 2002, in Chelan, Washington, an unattended campfire went wildly out of control. Within two days, 700 people had to be evacuated from the areas surrounding the fire. One week later, on July 22, the fire had spread to 20,992 acres (8,495 ha) and was only 10 percent contained. Nearly 1,000 personnel, twenty-six hand crews, four helicopters, sixty-four fire engines, eleven water tenders, and eight bulldozers were working on the fire as it continued to spread because of bad wind conditions.

Dipping low over a lake in Manson, Washington, on July 23, 2002, this helicopter fills up a huge bin of water to help fight the Deer Point Fire.

By July 24, the fire had burned 25,300 acres (10,239 ha). The night before, thunderstorms moved through the area and made the fire pick up activity. By then, 1,130 personnel, twenty-five hand crews, eight helicopters, and fifty-seven fire engines were on hand battling the blaze. Even with all that help, 32 more miles (51 km) of fire lines had to be built.

By August 19, 2002, the Deer Point Fire was 75 percent contained, but it now spanned 42,665 acres (17,266 ha). The fire was 100 percent contained by the end of August. It cost around $20 million to fight.

Sequoia National Park, California

The Sequoia National Park in Kernville, California, lies south of the Sierra Nevada mountain range. The forest is named for the giant sequoia trees that grow there. The sequoias are the largest trees on earth and are also some of the oldest. One sequoia tree can live more than 3,200 years. The park itself has more than 34,000 acres (13,759 ha) of sequoias and is the largest forest of sequoias in the world. The forest is considered a national treasure.

Unfortunately, the Sequoia National Park is also a hot spot for forest fires. Every year, about 200 fires break out in the forest, with 67 percent of them started by lightning. For firefighters, the Sequoia National Park is an extremely hard landscape in which to fight fires. The forest is very close to Bakersfield, California, and other towns. Plus, the landscape of the forest is full of deep canyons and ravines. The Deer Fire, which happened very close to the Sequoia National Park in Lake Isabella, California, is an example of how fast firefighters can gain control of a forest fire. In contrast, the McNally Fire would prove to be especially challenging for firefighters.

Deer Fire

The Deer Fire began around 10:30 PM on July 21, 2002. Forest officials determined that it was caused by humans but are still unsure of exactly how the fire started. Dry weather did cause the fire to spread quickly,

This man is dwarfed by a giant sequoia in Sequoia National Park, California. Sequoias are among the oldest living things on earth.

but a team of 435 firefighters and other personnel was able to battle the flames just as fast. By July 24, the fire was 100 percent contained. More than 1,800 acres (784 ha) burned in the Deer Fire.

McNally Fire

Firefighters were not so lucky containing the McNally Fire. This fire also began on July 21, when an unattended campfire turned into an out-of-control forest fire. By July 23, ten buildings had burned and so had 9,140 acres (3,699 ha) of treasured land. In one

These firefighters chart the progress of the McNally Fire burning in Sequoia National Park in Kernville, California. Covering 58,500 acres (23,674 ha) by July 26, 2002, the fire came very close to destroying the ancient sequoia trees.

day, the fire destroyed more than 1,600 acres (647 ha) and forced the evacuation of more than 1,000 people from their homes. The fire also threatened two major monuments: the Giant Sequoia National Monument and the park's Trail of 100 Giants. The fire was contained by the end of August, but not before it burned 15,000 acres (6,070 ha) of forest. The McNally Fire is the largest wildfire to ever happen in Sequoia National Park.

Winter and Toolbox Complex Fires, Oregon

On July 12, a lightning bolt sparked the beginning of the Winter Fire near the town of Paisley, Oregon. The fire was immediately spotted, but unfortunately, it still grew out of control. Oregon was experiencing droughtlike conditions during the summer of 2002 that

THE PULASKI: SIMPLE GENIUS

In 1910, Ed Pulaski thought of a way to combine an ax and a hand hoe into one tool. His invention is considered a major contribution to wildland firefighting. The tool, called a Pulaski after its inventor, is one of the oldest and most ingenious tools of wildland firefighting. The Pulaski is both an ax and a hoe. The ax side allows firefighters to cut trees and limbs, while the hoe side lets firefighters dig and scrape. Today, the Pulaski is still one of the basic tools used by wildland firefighters.

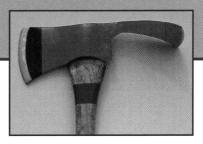

With Pulaski in hand, firefighter Dave Osborn monitors the progress of the Winter Fire in Summer Lake, Oregon, on July 22, 2002. The Winter Fire would later spread and become part of the Toolbox Complex Fire.

allowed the fire to spread at maximum speed. The Toolbox Fire was sparked by a thunderstorm just three days later. It started in Fremont National Forest and spread even faster than the Winter Fire. On July 17, the Federal Emergency Management Agency (FEMA) granted funds to the state of Oregon to help manage the fire.

Though firefighters were making headway on both blazes, the two fires merged into one huge blaze about ten days after they began. By July 24, the Toolbox Complex Fire had grown to about 50,000 acres (20,234 ha) and the Winter Fire was around 30,000 acres (12,141 ha).

With both fires combined, Oregon firefighters were trying to battle an 80,000-acre (32,375-ha) blaze. By then, four helicopters, seventy-nine fire engines, twenty-five bulldozers, and more than 2,000 people were fighting the merged fires. By late June, the merged fires were contained at just 40 percent, meaning that 60 percent of the fire line still needed to be built.

Both fires were put out by the end of August but not without significant damage to the Fremont National Forest. The Toolbox Complex Fire destroyed 95,012 acres (38,450 ha) of preserved forest while the Winter Fire destroyed an additional 32,000 acres (12,950 ha). The total cost of fighting both fires was around $10 million.

FIREFIGHTERS' HAND TOOLS

Most of the hand tools used by firefighters are combination tools. According to the National Fire News Agency, these hand tools must be effective, efficient, versatile, portable, simple, easy to maintain and repair, and able to be transported quickly.

The McLeod is a heavy-duty rake and hoe tool. The ax is used for cutting trees and branches. The shovel is a combination tool. Its edges are sharpened so that the user can chop down small trees and cut branches and roots. Firefighters also use shovels to scrape away pine needles and other duff (material on the forest floor) as they construct fire lines down to mineral soil, the soil that lies beneath duff.

Fire Season 2002: Colorado, Utah, and Arizona

In 2002, Arizona, Colorado, and Utah recorded their largest wildfires in a century. Both Colorado and Arizona witnessed the largest forest fires in the history of the states. Tragically, some firefighters lost their lives trying to control these blazes.

Hayman Fire, Colorado

The Hayman Fire, mentioned in chapter one, sounds like it could be made up: Terry Barton, a devoted Colorado forest worker, burns a love letter from her ex-husband in the forest. The letter ignites a huge forest fire that spreads to 137,760 acres (55,749 ha). It becomes the largest wildfire in Colorado's history.

The Hayman Fire was actually named for the Hayman site, an area near Tappan Gulch at the fire's origin. The fire was started on June 2, 2002, and was reported at 4 PM that afternoon by Barton, whose job was to spot illegal fires. The fire quickly spread out of control because of extremely dry weather conditions.

Mark Michelsen also worked on the Hayman Fire from the nearby Jeffco Airtanker Base. In his interview, he echoes the USDA

Forest Service, "Due to the size and complexity of this fire and the multiple fire suppression aircraft, coordination was very tough at times. At the Jeffco Airtanker Base, I had as many as twelve aircraft, at any time. Fire behavior was very extreme and often-times unpredictable. We were not able to fly due to many safety concerns, especially the fire activity. Also, with the type of unpredictable fire behavior, retardant would not have been effective in aiding in suppression of this fire."

Terry Barton was inadvertently responsible for starting the largest forest fire in the history of the state of Colorado. Barton is currently serving a prison sentence for starting the fire.

The fire was 100 percent contained by July 2—a month after it began. More than 130 homes were lost because of the fire, and many forest animals were displaced, or lost their homes.

FIRE SEASON 2002: THE STATS

By State	Number of Acres Burned
Alaska	2,191,280 (886,780 hectares)
Arizona	649,020 (262,649 ha)
California	426,496 (172, 597 ha)
Colorado	505,915 (204,737 ha)
Idaho	67,576 (27,347 ha)
Nevada	81,365 (32,927 ha)
New Mexico	308,244 (124,742 ha)
Oregon	992,475 (401,640 ha)
Utah	261,930 (105,999 ha)
Wyoming	76,208 (30,840 ha)
Total:	5,560,509 (2,250,258 ha)

Rattle Complex Fire, Utah

On June 20, 2002, a huge thunderstorm moved through Utah, 20 miles (32 km) northeast of Green River. The storm brought heavy lightning to the area and started two fires, the Diamond Fire and the Black Canyon Fire. Both fires together created the Rattle Complex Fire.

The Diamond Fire quickly spread, and by the end of July it had burned around 90,000 acres (36,421 ha). Crown fires were a big problem with the Diamond Fire and made it very hard for firefighters to control the southern part of the fire. The Black Canyon Fire was much smaller, at around 6,000 acres (2,428 ha). Both fires were 100 percent contained by early August.

Tragedy During the Battle for Big Elk, Colorado

On July 17, 2002, in the Arapahoe-Roosevelt National Forest, a fire began because of human activity. More than 650 people had to evacuate their homes because of the 4,000-acre (1,619-ha) Big Elk Fire. On July 18, an air tanker crashed into the blaze. Both men aboard were killed in the crash. Two weeks later on July 30, another helicopter went down, this time taking the life of another pilot. The tragedies were stark reminders that firefighting is dangerous work and that forest fires are treacherous.

Two pilots were killed when tanker 123 crashed over the Big Elk Fire while preparing to drop fire retardant over it.

Rodeo-Chediski Fire, Arizona

In northeastern Arizona on June 18, 2002, a fire broke out close to the Rodeo Fairgrounds on the Fort Apache Reservation. That night the fire was only about 100 to 300 acres (41 to 121 ha), but by the afternoon of June 20, the Rodeo Fire had grown to 30,000 acres (12,141 ha). Just fifteen miles away, another fire broke out near Chediski Peak when a lost hiker built a fire to signal for help. Within two days, the Rodeo and Chediski Fires merged and exploded into a 235,000-acre (95,101 ha) wildfire. By July, the Rodeo-Chediski Fire was at an astounding 500,000 acres (202,343 ha), making it the largest wildfire in the history of Arizona. For a fire this large, a huge number of resources were needed. There were 4,177 firefighters, twenty-six helicopters, 216 engines, 118 bulldozers, 101 water tenders, and twelve air tankers.

President George W. Bush declared the area a federal disaster area on June 26, 2002. Amazingly, the fire was 100 percent contained in less than a month—a great show of teamwork.

This Red Cross worker talks to people who have been evacuated from their homes because of the Rodeo-Chediski Fire on June 24, 2002.

Firefighters' Success and Teamwork

Wildland firefighting takes a strong team of people. Each fire is a disaster in itself, but preparation, organization, good strategy, and a tremendous amount of hard work help minimize the damage of any fire.

In 2002, firefighters did a great job suppressing fires because they suppressed 99 percent of all fires during their initial attack. Of the more than 70,000 fires reported, only about 610 became large.

This air tanker flies low over Forest Lakes, Arizona, spewing fire retardant from its cargo hold on June 26, 2002. The Rodeo-Chediski Fire was the worst forest fire in Arizona history.

At the end of the fire season, every firefighter is tired and ready for a break. Mark Michelsen knows firefighting is about relationships and teamwork, but it is also about support: "The best thing about my job is the people I work with. My loading crews and pilots become extended family during the fire season. Many of these pilots who fly these aircraft are the stuff legends and folktales are made from. They do a tough job that is very dangerous and sometimes fatal. Another thing that makes my job great is the support of my family."

The Future of Fire Seasons

In 2002, the Bush administration created a plan called the Healthy Forests Initiative. The initiative is up for debate among fire experts because it concentrates on thinning forests of dead and rotted tress, which provide fuel for fires. The plan does step up efforts to prevent forest fires, including giving more money for resources and forest fire prevention plans. However, some experts do not agree with thinning forests, believing that this course of

FOREST FIRE PREVENTION TIPS

From the National Fire News Agency, the following tips are helpful in preventing forest fires:

- Never park a vehicle on dry grass.
- Never throw a lit cigarette out the window of a vehicle.
- Never play with matches, lighters, flammable liquids, or any fire.
- When building a campfire, clear the campfire site down to bare soil.
- Circle all campfire pits with rocks.
- Build campfires away from overhanging branches, steep slopes, dry grass, and leaves.
- Always have an adult around to supervise outdoor cooking.
- Never leave a campfire unattended.
- When putting out a campfire, drown the fire, stir it, and drown it again.
- Be careful with gas lanterns, barbecues, gas stoves, and anything that can be a source of ignition for a wildfire.
- Tell your friends about fire prevention.

President Bush, seen here in the Oval Office on December 11, 2002, is going ahead with a controversial fire-prevention plan that involves thinning the country's forests. Environmental groups claim that the plan actually allows wholesale logging of old-growth trees and national forests.

action would promote unsound logging practices. To read more about the controversial Healthy Forests Initiative, please see the For More Information section at the back of this book.

Overall, the fire season is still a major problem every year in the United States. Hundreds of thousands of firefighters give their time, energy, and passion to putting out these forest fires as fast as they can.

If firefighters, fire ecologists, wildlife societies, politicians, and communities work together like firefighters do as they battle the blazes, future fire seasons may not be as harmful and dangerous to the ecosystem.

Timeline

August–November 1999
The Big Bar Complex Fire in California burns more than 140,947 acres (57,039 hectares).

September–November 1999
In the Kirk Complex Fire in California, around 86,700 acres (35,086 ha) burn after three months of intense firefighting.

May–July 2000
The Cerro Grande Fire becomes the worst in New Mexico history when it burns around 50,000 acres (20,234 ha) of forest.

June 2000
Near Denver, Colorado, the Bobcat Gulch and Hi Meadows Fires burn nearly 11,000 acres (4,452 ha) of forest.

July–September 2000
The Bitterroot Valley Fires are started by lightning in Montana and engulf more than 300,000 acres (121,406 ha) of land.

July–October 2000
The Clear Creek Fire in Idaho is started by lightning and destroys 206,500 acres (83,568 ha) of forest.

July 2001
The Thirtymile Fire in Washington is started by a cooking fire. Four firefighters are killed before the blaze is contained.

August–September 2001
Lightning starts the Lakeview Complex Fire in Oregon, destroying 127,552 acres (51,618 ha) in just seven days.

June–July 2002

The Rodeo-Chediski Fire becomes the largest fire in the history of Arizona; a Colorado forest worker starts the Hayman Fire, which becomes the worst forest fire in the history of Colorado.

June–August 2002

The Deer Point Fire in Washington burns 42,665 acres (17,266 ha). In Utah, two fires merge to become the Rattle Complex Fire, which burns nearly 100,000 acres (40,469 ha).

July–August 2002

On July 13, 2002, the Biscuit Fire breaks out in southern Oregon and eventually stretches into northern California. Estimated to be one of Oregon's largest forest fires in recorded history, it reaches 499,965 acres (202,239 ha).

July–August 2002

The Big Elk Fire in Colorado takes the lives of three firefighters. The McNally and Deer Fires start on the same day. The fires burn a significant amount of the Sequoia National Park in California. The Toolbox Complex Fire and the Winter Fire destroy around 120,000 acres (48,562 ha) of Oregon's forests.

August 2002

President George W. Bush begins promoting the new Healthy Forests Initiative, which will focus on thinning forests to prevent uncontrollable forest fires. The move draws criticism from environmentalists.

2003

According to the National Interagency Fire Center, the 2003 fire season is significantly below average. However, enormous fires rage through parts of Arizona, Idaho, Montana, and Oregon.

Glossary

acre (AY-ker) A unit of measure used to figure out land size; one acre is about the size of a football field.

aerial firefighter (EHR-ee-uhl FYR-FIH-tur) A firefighter who works from the air and usually pilots an air tanker.

air tanker (AYR TAN-kur) An airplane used in fighting forest fires; the plane has huge bins that carry fire retardant to drop onto the fire.

arson (AR-sun) The act of starting a fire intentionally.

dissipate (DIS-sip-AYT) To spread, thin out, and gradually vanish.

duff (DUFF) Organic material lining a forest floor.

ecosystem (EE-koh-SIS-tem) A community of plant and animals functioning together.

fire ecologist (FYR ee-KAH-luh-jist) Scientist who studies forest fires.

fire line (FYR LYN) A trench built around a fire to contain it; it can be natural, like a river, or man-made, like a road.

fire suppression policy (FYR suh-PREH-shun PAH-lih-see) The strategy that fire ecologists use to approach the fire season, both before and during it.

hotshot (HAHTSHOT) A firefighter who builds fire lines and firebreaks.

hot spot (HAHT SPAHT) A small fire that starts when the main fire is almost put out; usually happens after the fire line is built.

perimeter (pe-RIM-ee-tur) The outer limit or surrounding area.

For More Information

Federal Wildland Fire Service Association
P.O. Box 2232
Nevada City, CA 95959
(916) 274-1159
Web site: http://www.fwfsa.org

USDA Forest Service
P.O. Box 96090
Washington, DC 20090-6090
(202) 205-8333
e-mail: wo_fs-contact@fs.fed.us
Web site: http://www.fs.fed.us

Web Sites

Due to the changing nature of Internet links, the Rosen Publishing Group, Inc., has developed an online list of Web sites related to the subject of this book. This site is updated regularly. Please use this link to access the list:

http://www.rosenlinks.com/tfth/ffwu

For Further Reading

Beil, Karen Magnuson. *Fire in Their Eyes: Wildfires and the People Who Fight Them*. New York: Harcourt, 1999.

Beyer, Mark. *Smokejumpers: Life Fighting Fires*. New York: Rosen Publishing Group, 2001.

Cone, Patrick. *Wildfire*. Minneapolis: Carolrhoda Books, 1996.

Patent, Dorothy Hinshaw. *Fire: Friend or Foe*. New York: Clarion Books, 1998.

Salas, Laura Purdie. *Forest Fires*. Montaka, MN: Capstone Press, 2001.

Thompson, Luke. *Forest Fires*. Danbury, CT: Children's Press, 2000.

Bibliography

"Fact Sheet: The Healthy Forests Initiative." Office of the Press Secretary, White House, August 2002. Retrieved February 5, 2003 (http://www.whitehouse.gov/news/releases/2002/08/20020821-2.html).

"FEMA Authorizes Funds for Second Oregon Wildfire." FEMA, July 17, 2002. Retrieved February 5, 2003 (http://www.fema.gov/diz02/hq02_113.shtm).

Foster, Dick. "Hi Meadow Fire 'Human-caused.'" *Rocky Mountain News*, June 21, 2000. Retrieved February 5, 2003 (http://denver.rockymountainnews.com/news/0621fire1.shtml).

"Hayman Fire and BAER Information Incident Report." USDA Forest Service, April 23, 2003. Retrieved February 23, 2003 (http://www.fs.fed.us/r2/psicc/hayres/index.htm).

"Hi Meadows Fire." USDA Forest Service, April 24, 2003. Retrieved February 5, 2003 (http://www.fs.fed.us/r2/psicc/spl/himead.shtml).

"Major Fires in the West: A Guide to the Fire Season's Destruction." CNN, July 24, 2002. Retrieved February 7, 2003 (http://www.cnn.com/2002/US/07/23/wildfires.glance/?related).

Michelsen, Mark A. E-mail interview by author. Bloomfield, CO, April 18, 2003.

Solomon, Chris. "Why Thirty Mile Fire Raged Without Water." The *Seattle Times*, August 1, 2001. Retrieved April 7, 2003 (http://seattletimes.nwsource.com/html/localnews/134324629_fishfire01m.html).

Index

About the Author

Katherine White is a freelance writer and editor in and around New York City. She lives in Jersey City, New Jersey.

Acknowledgments

The author would like to thank Mark A. Michelsen for his time and his expert contributions to this book—your help is much appreciated. Ron, thanks for the inspiration.

Photo Credits

Cover, p. 1 © John McColgan/BLM AK Fire Service; pp. 5, 22, 24, 26, 28, 30, 33, 38, 40 ©AP/Wide World Photos; pp. 8, 27 © Phil Schermeister/Corbis; p. 9 © Image Club Graphics; p. 13 © Barry Gutierrez/Rocky Mountain News, June 26, 2002/Reprinted with permission of the Rocky Mountain News; p. 14 © Gregory Ochocki/Photo Researchers, Inc.: pp. 19, 37 © Reuters NewMedia Inc./Corbis; pp. 20, 23 Mark Michelsen; p. 21 AFP/Corbis; p. 29 © Mike McMillan; p. 36 © Matt Inden/Denver Rocky Mountain News/Corbis

Designer: Les Kanturek; Editor: Charles Hofer; Photo Researcher: Amy Feinberg